A Beginner's Guide to Artificial Intelligence

Preface

We live in an era where Artificial Intelligence (AI) is no longer a futuristic concept confined to science fiction, but a tangible reality that permeates many facets of our daily lives. From personalized product recommendations in online stores to AI-assisted medical diagnostics, from self-driving vehicles to the spam filters in our inboxes, AI is rapidly changing how we interact with the world.

This book is born from the need to offer a comprehensive and accessible view of Artificial Intelligence—both to newcomers curious about its foundations and to more experienced readers seeking to delve deeper into its applications, technical underpinnings, and ethical and societal implications. Our goal is not only to describe the current state of this technology, but also to equip readers with the tools to understand where this field may lead us in the future.

The structure of this volume follows a logical and progressive path. Early sections begin by defining AI and discussing its historical roots, then move on to explore the various types of AI and their key subfields—such as Machine Learning, Deep Learning, Computer Vision, and Natural Language Processing. Building on this, the text delves into the core technical foundations, algorithms, programming languages, and development platforms, providing a holistic overview of the tools and workflows required to bring real-world AI projects to life.

Special attention is given to practical applications. Sectors such as healthcare, finance, automotive, manufacturing, and creative industries illustrate how AI is not merely an academic pursuit, but a transformative force reshaping entire economic and social landscapes. At the same time, we do not overlook the delicate issues surrounding ethics, privacy, accountability, and the potential impact of intelligent automation on the labor market.

Subsequent chapters guide readers in acquiring the basic skills needed to experiment on their own. We highlight educational resources, recommended development environments, and practical exercises to help readers put their newly acquired knowledge into practice. We then conclude with a forward-looking perspective on the future of AI, considering both near- and long-term scenarios—speculating on the development of more sophisticated or even general intelligence systems, and reflecting on their far-reaching societal implications.

In such a dynamic and rapidly evolving field, this book's aim is to serve as a compass, guiding readers through the broad landscape of Artificial Intelligence and providing the insights needed to understand its mechanisms, significance, advantages, and potential pitfalls. We hope that these pages inspire curiosity, critical thinking, and a desire to contribute positively to the transformative journey that lies ahead.

Published by NEXUS LINK LLC

First edition: November 2024

ISBN: 9798303960039

Cover design by Nexus Link LLC

1. Introduction to Artificial Intelligence
- **What is Artificial Intelligence?**
    - Definition of AI
    - A brief history of AI: From early computing to modern AI advancements
- **The Importance and Impact of AI in Contemporary Society**
    - How AI is transforming the world (everyday examples)
    - Opportunities and challenges posed by AI
- **Goals of this Book**
    - Why learn about AI?
    - Book structure and content overview

2. Types of Artificial Intelligence
- **Narrow AI vs General AI**
    - Differences between specific and general AI
    - Current research state on Artificial General Intelligence (AGI)
- **Artificial Intelligence vs Machine Learning**
    - Definition of Machine Learning (ML)
    - Distinctions between AI and ML
- **AI Subfields in Depth**
    - **Machine Learning**: Models that learn from data
    - **Deep Learning**: Advanced neural networks
    - **Natural Language Processing (NLP)**: Language analysis
    - **Computer Vision**: Image recognition and analysis
    - **Robotics and Physical AI**: AI's interaction with physical devices

3. Technical Foundations of Artificial Intelligence
- **Core Machine Learning Algorithms**
    - Supervised and unsupervised algorithms
    - Neural networks and backpropagation
- **Fundamentals of Deep Learning**
    - Neural network architectures

- o Convolution and convolutional neural networks (CNN)
- **AI Programming Languages and Platforms**
  - o Python and its main libraries (TensorFlow, PyTorch, Scikit-Learn)
  - o Overview of major AI platforms and cloud providers (Google AI, AWS, Azure AI)
- **AI Project Pipeline**
  - o Steps to build an AI project: from raw data to functional models
  - o Importance of data collection and cleaning

4. Real-World Applications of AI
- **AI in Everyday Life**
  - o Virtual assistants, social media, search engines
- **AI in Various Industries**
  - o **Healthcare**: Assisted diagnostics, personalized medicine
  - o **Finance**: Risk management, algorithmic trading
  - o **Automotive**: Autonomous driving and driver assistance
  - o **Retail and e-Commerce**: Recommendations, customer personalization
  - o **Manufacturing**: Predictive maintenance, automation
- **AI in Creativity**
  - o Automated content generation (text, images, music)
  - o AI in film and artistic production

5. Ethics and Considerations in AI
- **Risks and Challenges of AI**
  - o Algorithmic bias and discrimination
  - o AI security and potential threats
- **Privacy and Data Security**
  - o Protection of personal data
  - o Ethical and legal data management
- **AI and Employment**
  - o AI's impact on jobs
  - o New skills and preparation for the future

- **AI Regulation**
  - International and local AI regulations
  - Prospects for AI regulatory frameworks

6. Getting Started with Artificial Intelligence
- **Resources for Learning AI**
  - Recommended online courses, tutorials, and books
  - Online communities, forums, and blogs
- **Beginner-Friendly Development Tools**
  - Installing Python and using primary libraries
  - Basic AI projects to start (simple ML models for beginners)
- **Hands-On Exercises and Mini-Projects**
  - Step-by-step guide for small ML projects (e.g., prediction, classification)
  - Ideas for personal projects to deepen knowledge

7. The Future of Artificial Intelligence
- **Current Trends in AI**
  - Progress in advanced neural networks and explainable AI
  - AI in quantum computing
- **Vision for AI's Future**
  - What AGI could mean for society
  - Optimistic and pessimistic scenarios
- **Conclusion and Final Reflections**
  - Summary of key concepts covered
  - How AI will reshape the world: personal and global implications

Appendices and Additional Resources
- **Glossary of Technical Terms**
  - Definitions of useful technical terms for beginners
- **Recommended Resources**
  - Books, courses, websites, and videos for further exploration
- **Practice Exercises and Quizzes**
  - Practical exercises for comprehension checks
  - Summary quizzes for each chapter

Chapter 1
Introduction to Artificial Intelligence

What is Artificial Intelligence?

Artificial Intelligence, often abbreviated as AI, is the branch of computer science dedicated to creating systems capable of performing tasks that typically require human intelligence. These tasks range from simple functions like recognizing speech or images to complex processes such as decision-making, learning, and language understanding. Essentially, AI encompasses a vast array of technologies that aim to mimic or replicate cognitive functions associated with the human mind.

Definition of AI

AI can be defined as the simulation of human intelligence in machines, allowing them to perform tasks that would normally require human cognition. This broad definition encompasses various subfields, such as machine learning, natural language processing, and robotics, each contributing unique techniques and applications to the field. Today's AI technologies leverage algorithms and computational power to solve complex problems, adapt to new data, and continuously improve their performance.

A Brief History of AI: From Early Computers to Modern AI

The story of AI is intertwined with the history of computing itself. In the 1950s, the concept of machines capable of mimicking human thought began to emerge among pioneering computer scientists. The early theoretical groundwork was laid by researchers such as Alan Turing, who famously proposed the Turing Test, a method to evaluate a machine's ability to exhibit intelligent behavior indistinguishable from that of a human. However, these early ideas remained largely hypothetical due to technological limitations of the time.

In the 1980s, the development of neural networks, inspired by the architecture of the human brain, reignited interest in AI research. Although progress was slow, these networks laid the foundation for modern machine learning. With the advent of faster processors and the exponential growth of data in the 2000s, AI experienced a resurgence. Today, we live in the age of "deep learning," a form of AI that leverages large amounts of data to enable machines to perform tasks like image recognition and language processing with remarkable accuracy.

In the span of just a few decades, AI has evolved from theoretical discussions to practical applications, shaping industries from healthcare to finance, and influencing everyday life through smart devices, search engines, and personalized recommendations. The future promises even more advancements, where AI might surpass human capabilities in specific domains, sparking both excitement and ethical considerations.

The Importance and Impact of AI in Contemporary Society
Artificial Intelligence (AI) is no longer a distant technological dream; it has become an integral part of our daily lives, subtly transforming how we work, interact, and make decisions. In just a few decades, AI has evolved from a niche field within computer science to a driver of change across industries, redefining norms in healthcare, finance, education, and beyond. This section explores AI's significance in today's society, examining both its everyday applications and its broader social implications.

How AI is Changing the World (Everyday Examples)
AI has become so embedded in our daily routines that many of us may not even realize we interact with it regularly. Here are a few common examples of how AI is reshaping everyday life:

- **Personalized Recommendations**: From streaming services like Netflix and Spotify to online shopping platforms such as Amazon, AI algorithms analyze user preferences and behaviors to suggest content and products tailored to individual tastes.
- **Voice-Activated Assistants**: Assistants like Siri, Alexa, and Google Assistant use natural language processing (NLP) to interpret and respond to voice commands, helping users with tasks from setting reminders to controlling smart home devices.
- **Smart Transportation**: AI in navigation apps (like Google Maps) provides real-time traffic updates and optimal routes, making travel more efficient. Autonomous vehicles, although still in development, promise to reduce accidents and traffic

congestion by using machine learning and computer vision to "see" and react to the road environment.

- **Healthcare Support**: AI aids doctors in diagnosing diseases, analyzing patient data, and recommending treatments, allowing for quicker and often more accurate medical decisions. Wearable devices use AI to monitor vital signs and detect potential health issues, helping individuals manage their health proactively.

These examples illustrate that AI is not confined to laboratories or high-tech sectors; it is woven into the fabric of daily life, enhancing convenience, personalization, and efficiency.

Opportunities and Challenges Presented by AI

AI offers immense opportunities to advance society by addressing complex challenges, improving productivity, and enhancing decision-making processes. However, it also brings several challenges that require thoughtful consideration.

- **Opportunities**:
  - **Enhanced Productivity**: AI can handle repetitive tasks and analyze large datasets quickly, enabling humans to focus on creative and strategic work. In industries like manufacturing and customer service, AI-driven automation has streamlined operations and reduced costs.
  - **Better Decision-Making**: By analyzing trends and patterns in vast amounts of data, AI can provide insights that support better decision-making in fields like finance, healthcare, and environmental conservation.
  - **Healthcare Innovation**: AI's ability to process complex medical data aids in early diagnosis, personalized treatments, and drug discovery, potentially revolutionizing patient care and reducing mortality rates.
  - **Environmental Protection**: AI models analyze climate data to predict weather patterns, assess risks, and contribute to sustainable development efforts. For example, AI-powered monitoring systems can track

deforestation and poaching activities, helping
conservation efforts.

- **Challenges**:
  - ○ **Privacy and Security Concerns**: AI systems often
    require vast amounts of personal data to operate
    effectively. This data dependency raises questions
    about privacy, data security, and potential misuse of
    information.
  - ○ **Bias and Fairness**: Since AI models learn from data,
    they can inadvertently reinforce societal biases
    present in the data. This bias in algorithms can lead to
    unfair treatment, particularly in areas like hiring,
    lending, and law enforcement.
  - ○ **Impact on Employment**: AI-driven automation
    threatens to replace certain jobs, especially in sectors
    like manufacturing, retail, and transportation. While
    AI creates new opportunities, reskilling the workforce
    to adapt to AI-driven roles remains a pressing issue.
  - ○ **Ethical Dilemmas**: As AI systems grow in capability,
    ethical questions surrounding their decision-making
    processes become more significant. For example,
    autonomous vehicles must be programmed to make
    ethical decisions in scenarios where human lives are
    at risk.

In summary, AI's impact on contemporary society is profound,
offering new opportunities while posing unique challenges. The way
AI is managed and integrated will shape the future, making it crucial
for society to address these challenges thoughtfully.

Objectives of the eBook

As technology rapidly evolves, Artificial Intelligence has become
essential knowledge across a wide range of industries, from
healthcare to finance, and even in creative fields like art and design.
This eBook is designed to provide a clear and engaging introduction
to AI for beginners, presenting its key concepts, potential

applications, and the fundamental skills needed to understand and even begin using AI tools.

Why Learn AI?
AI is not just a trending topic; it's a transformative force shaping the future. Learning about AI is valuable for several reasons:
   1. **Career Opportunities**
AI knowledge is increasingly in demand, as companies worldwide seek skilled professionals who understand machine learning, data science, and automation. Whether one is interested in a technical role, a management position, or even a career in a non-technical field, AI skills can provide a competitive edge.
   2. **Adaptability and Future-Proofing**
As AI reshapes entire industries, understanding its principles can help individuals prepare for future changes in their jobs. AI literacy enables people to adapt to shifts in technology, better understand new tools, and even make informed decisions about implementing AI in their own work.
   3. **Critical Thinking and Ethical Awareness**
Learning about AI goes beyond technical skills. It encourages critical thinking about ethical issues, such as privacy, job automation, and algorithmic bias. By understanding AI, readers can better navigate the ethical implications of technology in both personal and professional settings.

Structure and Contents of the Book
This eBook is structured to gradually guide readers from fundamental concepts to practical applications, making it accessible to those without prior knowledge of AI. The layout aims to introduce complex ideas in an engaging and understandable way, balancing technical insights with real-world examples.
   • **Foundational Concepts**
Readers will first explore the fundamental ideas of AI, including definitions, types, and technical terminology. These concepts build a base that will be expanded upon in later chapters.
   • **Technical Underpinnings**
To provide a deeper understanding, the eBook covers the core technologies behind AI, such as machine learning algorithms, neural

networks, and natural language processing, all explained with clarity.

- **Practical Applications**

The book explores the wide range of AI applications across various industries, showing readers how AI impacts their daily lives and future professions. This section provides both current examples and potential future uses.

- **Ethical and Societal Implications**

AI comes with significant ethical considerations, from data privacy to employment impacts. This section encourages readers to think critically about these issues, equipping them with the knowledge to make informed decisions about AI use.

- **Resources and Exercises**

Finally, the book includes resources, exercises, and project ideas for readers who wish to apply what they've learned, making the eBook both a learning guide and a springboard for practical exploration. By the end, readers will have a holistic understanding of AI, empowering them to make informed choices and explore opportunities in this dynamic field.

Goal: Demonstrate a basic rule-based decision to highlight the difference between static logic and more advanced AI capabilities. Although not "true AI," it helps introduce the idea of machines making decisions.

Example:

```python
# A simple if-statement simulating a "decision"
weather = "rainy"
if weather == "rainy":
    print("Carry an umbrella.")
else:
    print("No umbrella needed.")
```

Chapter 2
Types of Artificial Intelligence

Types of Artificial Intelligence

As Artificial Intelligence evolves, it has branched into different types, each with varying capabilities, applications, and goals. These types reflect the range of intelligence levels that AI can reach, from specialized systems capable of performing specific tasks to ambitious goals of creating machines that could potentially think and learn like humans. This chapter introduces two main types of AI: Weak AI, or Narrow AI, and Strong AI, or General AI, explaining their fundamental differences and the current state of research on Artificial General Intelligence (AGI).

Weak AI (Narrow AI) vs. Strong AI (General AI)

- **Weak AI (Narrow AI)**: This type of AI, often referred to as Narrow AI, is designed and trained to perform a specific task or a limited set of tasks. For example, a speech recognition system, like the one used in digital assistants, can understand and respond to voice commands but cannot perform any function outside of that domain. Narrow AI is widely used today and excels at handling specialized tasks, making it the most common form of AI present in everyday technology. These systems are not "intelligent" in a human sense; they operate within a narrow, defined range and cannot adapt to entirely new tasks without reprogramming or retraining.
- **Strong AI (General AI)**: Unlike Narrow AI, Strong AI, or General AI, aspires to replicate human-like intelligence, where a machine can understand, learn, and apply knowledge across a variety of domains autonomously. In theory, an AGI system would be capable of reasoning, making decisions, and learning in the same manner as a human, applying insights from one field to solve problems in unrelated areas. The development of AGI remains a theoretical goal, and achieving it would require breakthroughs that allow machines to develop deep, cross-functional cognitive skills. Today, General AI remains largely hypothetical, and researchers continue to debate both the feasibility and the

ethical implications of achieving human-like intelligence in machines.

Current State of Research on AGI (Artificial General Intelligence)

The pursuit of AGI has attracted immense interest from both researchers and industry leaders, sparking philosophical, technical, and ethical debates. Unlike Narrow AI, which is already well integrated into various fields, AGI demands innovations in several key areas:

- **Computational Power**: AGI would require unprecedented levels of processing power, memory, and data handling capabilities to replicate complex human cognition.
- **Learning Algorithms**: While Narrow AI uses specialized algorithms for specific tasks, AGI would need algorithms that can generalize across disciplines and adapt to new situations without needing extensive reprogramming.
- **Ethical and Safety Concerns**: AGI, by nature, would have capabilities that require careful oversight to prevent unintended consequences. As such, safety measures and ethical considerations play a crucial role in AGI research. Leaders in AI are actively working on guidelines to ensure any advancements in AGI are aligned with human values and safety standards.

Despite advances in machine learning, computer vision, and natural language processing, AGI remains a long-term objective. While some experts believe it could be achieved within a few decades, others caution that true AGI may remain out of reach, limited by both technical and philosophical boundaries.

Artificial Intelligence and Machine Learning

As we dive deeper into the field of Artificial Intelligence (AI), it's essential to understand one of its most critical components: Machine Learning (ML). Although AI and ML are often used interchangeably, they refer to distinct concepts. This section defines Machine Learning, explains how it functions within the broader context of AI, and clarifies the differences between these two interconnected but separate domains.

Definition of Machine Learning (ML)
Machine Learning, or ML, is a subset of AI that focuses on enabling systems to learn from data, identify patterns, and make decisions with minimal human intervention. Rather than following explicitly programmed instructions, ML algorithms analyze large datasets to "learn" and improve over time. This learning process enables computers to predict outcomes, categorize information, and even adapt to new information without being manually adjusted for every change.
In more technical terms, ML relies on algorithms that iteratively train on data. The system continuously adjusts its parameters to achieve more accurate results as it processes additional information. For example, an ML model trained on thousands of email examples learns to detect spam by recognizing certain keywords, patterns, and sender behaviors. This learning capability is crucial for applications like image recognition, recommendation systems, language translation, and fraud detection.

Difference Between AI and ML
While Machine Learning is a subset of Artificial Intelligence, it's important to distinguish the two. AI refers to the broader field that encompasses any technology designed to emulate human intelligence, including reasoning, problem-solving, and decision-making. AI is an umbrella term, covering various approaches and methods aimed at achieving human-like cognition, from rule-based systems to complex neural networks.
Machine Learning, however, is specifically focused on the data-driven approach within AI. Unlike traditional AI that might follow preset rules, ML emphasizes learning from experience through data. While AI includes techniques that allow computers to act intelligently, ML specifically provides the methods by which

computers "learn" from past data to improve their performance. In short, all ML is AI, but not all AI is ML.

In practical terms, an AI system can be designed to play chess with a set of programmed rules. In contrast, an ML-based chess program would "learn" by analyzing countless moves, recognizing strategies, and adapting its gameplay based on experience. Thus, Machine Learning can be seen as a specific approach to achieving the broader goals of AI, particularly for tasks that benefit from continuous improvement and adaptation to new information.

In-depth Look at AI Subfields

Artificial Intelligence is not a single technology but a diverse field with numerous specialized branches. Among the most prominent subfields are **Machine Learning** and **Deep Learning**. These domains have become central to modern AI, powering everything from recommendation algorithms to voice recognition systems and complex data analysis tasks. This chapter explores these core areas, outlining how they function, their unique characteristics, and their impact on the AI landscape.

Machine Learning: Models That Learn from Data
Machine Learning (ML) is a subset of AI focused on developing algorithms that enable computers to learn from and make predictions or decisions based on data. In essence, ML enables systems to automatically improve their performance by recognizing patterns in data without being explicitly programmed for each task.

The concept of Machine Learning emerged in the mid-20th century, gaining momentum as researchers sought to create systems that could "learn" from experience. Unlike traditional software, which follows a set of pre-defined rules, ML algorithms use data to generate models that can make predictions or identify trends. For example:

- **Supervised Learning**: The system is trained on labeled data, where the input and desired output are known. This approach is commonly used in tasks like spam detection or credit scoring.

- **Unsupervised Learning**: The system finds hidden patterns or groupings in unlabeled data. It's often used in applications like market segmentation and customer profiling.
- **Reinforcement Learning**: The algorithm learns by interacting with an environment, receiving rewards or penalties based on its actions, which is the foundation for many game-playing AI systems.

Machine Learning has become an indispensable tool in today's world. Its applications range from email filtering and predictive maintenance to complex fields like medical diagnosis, where algorithms analyze vast datasets to assist doctors in identifying potential health risks.

Deep Learning: The Power of Neural Networks

Deep Learning (DL) is a specialized form of Machine Learning that utilizes neural networks with many layers – hence the term "deep" – to process vast amounts of data and make highly accurate predictions. Inspired by the human brain's neural networks, DL algorithms consist of interconnected layers of nodes that mimic neuron connections. This structure allows DL models to learn intricate patterns in data, handling complex tasks that are difficult for traditional ML models.

One of the key innovations in Deep Learning is the **Convolutional Neural Network** (CNN), designed specifically for image processing tasks. CNNs have become the cornerstone of facial recognition, autonomous driving, and medical image analysis by accurately identifying patterns in images, such as edges, colors, and shapes. Another critical model is the **Recurrent Neural Network** (RNN), which is effective for sequence-based data like language and time series, making it invaluable in applications like language translation and speech recognition.

Deep Learning has driven revolutionary changes in AI capabilities. Unlike traditional ML, which often requires carefully designed feature extraction, DL models can autonomously extract features, making them incredibly powerful for tasks with high-dimensional data. This capacity has expanded the possibilities for AI applications in various fields, such as:

- **Healthcare**: Assisting in detecting diseases from radiographic images

- **Finance**: Enhancing fraud detection by identifying subtle, complex patterns
- **Entertainment**: Powering recommendations on streaming platforms and personalizing user experiences

By pushing the boundaries of what AI systems can accomplish, Deep Learning has cemented itself as a critical component of modern AI, continuously pushing the limits of accuracy, adaptability, and automation.

In-Depth Exploration of AI Subfields

Artificial Intelligence encompasses various specialized subfields, each designed to address different aspects of human intelligence and cognition. These subfields allow AI to perform tasks that require advanced perception, language understanding, and physical interaction, making it possible for AI systems to interpret, interact with, and manipulate the world around them. This chapter delves into three primary subfields of AI that have become essential in modern applications: Natural Language Processing (NLP), Computer Vision, and Robotics.

Natural Language Processing (NLP): Language Analysis

Natural Language Processing, or NLP, focuses on enabling machines to understand, interpret, and respond to human language in a way that is both meaningful and useful. NLP allows AI systems to process written and spoken language, making it essential for applications ranging from voice-activated assistants to real-time translation tools.

1. **Understanding Human Language**: Human language is complex, with nuanced syntax, semantics, and context. NLP systems are designed to break down these layers, enabling AI to understand context, detect emotions, and even identify sarcasm or intent.
2. **Applications of NLP**: NLP powers many everyday technologies, such as:

- o **Voice Assistants** like Siri, Alexa, and Google Assistant, which understand and respond to voice commands.
- o **Machine Translation** services (like Google Translate), which interpret and translate text across different languages.
- o **Sentiment Analysis** in social media and customer feedback, helping businesses understand public opinion.
3. **Advancements in NLP**: Recent developments, such as large language models (like GPT-4), have made it possible for NLP systems to generate human-like text, engage in conversation, and assist in tasks like summarizing, writing, and coding. This progress has broadened the scope and sophistication of NLP applications.

Computer Vision: Image Recognition and Analysis

Computer Vision is a branch of AI focused on enabling machines to interpret and process visual data. This technology replicates a human's ability to recognize patterns, detect objects, and interpret images, making it a powerful tool in fields where visual analysis is critical.

1. **How Computer Vision Works**: Computer Vision uses techniques such as convolutional neural networks (CNNs) to analyze images, detect patterns, and make predictions. These models are trained on massive datasets, allowing them to recognize complex patterns and objects with high accuracy.
2. **Applications of Computer Vision**:
   - o **Medical Imaging**: Assists in diagnosing diseases through analysis of X-rays, MRIs, and CT scans.
   - o **Autonomous Vehicles**: Helps self-driving cars identify pedestrians, road signs, and other vehicles.
   - o **Security**: Used in facial recognition and surveillance to monitor and identify individuals.
3. **Future of Computer Vision**: As data availability and processing power continue to increase, Computer Vision is expected to evolve, enhancing its precision and ability to

make complex interpretations. These advancements may include interpreting emotions through facial expressions, real-time video analysis, and improving human-computer interactions.

Robotics and Physical AI: Interaction Between AI and Physical Devices

Robotics combines AI with physical systems, creating intelligent machines that can move, manipulate objects, and interact with their environments. This field is essential in industries requiring automation, precision, and real-time responsiveness, from manufacturing to healthcare.

1. **Robotics Components**:
   - **Sensors** allow robots to perceive their surroundings, detecting physical changes, obstacles, or temperatures.
   - **Actuators** are mechanical devices enabling movement, allowing robots to interact physically with objects or navigate spaces.
2. **Applications of Robotics**:
   - **Manufacturing and Automation**: Robots assemble products, perform repetitive tasks, and handle dangerous materials.
   - **Medical Robotics**: Used in surgery, rehabilitation, and patient monitoring, enhancing precision and safety.
   - **Agriculture**: Robots assist with planting, harvesting, and monitoring crop health.
3. **Robotics and AI Synergy**: The integration of AI enhances robots' ability to make decisions, respond to dynamic environments, and perform tasks with greater autonomy and accuracy. This synergy opens the door to advances in fields like autonomous drones, robotic prosthetics, and rescue operations in disaster zones.

Goal: Show an example of Narrow AI with a very simple machine learning model. Here, we use Logistic Regression to classify even/odd numbers—an artificial but illustrative scenario.

Example:

```python
import random
from sklearn.linear_model import LogisticRegression

# Generate data: numbers 0 to 99
X = [[i] for i in range(100)]
y = [0 if i % 2 == 0 else 1 for i in range(100)]  # 0=even, 1=odd

model = LogisticRegression()
model.fit(X, y)

print("Prediction for 42:", model.predict([[42]]))  # Should predict 0 (even
print("Prediction for 57:", model.predict([[57]]))  # Should predict 1 (odd)
```

Chapter 3
Technical Foundations of Artificial Intelligence

Technical Foundations of Artificial Intelligence

In this section, we delve into the core technical principles that underpin Artificial Intelligence, focusing on machine learning algorithms. Understanding these foundational algorithms is essential to comprehend how AI learns, adapts, and improves over time. Machine Learning (ML), a crucial subset of AI, enables systems to learn from data and make decisions with minimal human intervention. Here, we explore supervised and unsupervised learning, followed by an introduction to neural networks and the process of backpropagation.

Basic Machine Learning Algorithms

Machine learning relies on a series of algorithms that process data to recognize patterns, draw insights, and ultimately make decisions or predictions. These algorithms are generally divided into two main categories: supervised and unsupervised learning.

Supervised Learning Algorithms

In supervised learning, algorithms learn from a labeled dataset, meaning that each input has an associated output or "label." This method resembles how humans learn with guidance or examples. The algorithm uses these input-output pairs to understand relationships within the data, refining its model with each iteration to improve accuracy.

Some common supervised learning algorithms include:

- **Linear Regression:** Used for predicting continuous values based on the relationship between input and output variables.
- **Decision Trees:** These algorithms create a tree-like model of decisions, valuable for both classification and regression tasks.
- **Support Vector Machines (SVM):** This algorithm finds the optimal boundary (or hyperplane) that best separates classes within the data.

Unsupervised Learning Algorithms

In unsupervised learning, the algorithm works with data that has no labels, meaning it must find patterns, groupings, or structures within the dataset on its own. This method is particularly useful for tasks

like data clustering and dimensionality reduction, where we aim to reveal hidden structures or simplify data representation.
Some prominent unsupervised learning algorithms are:

- **K-Means Clustering:** This method divides the data into "clusters" based on feature similarity.
- **Principal Component Analysis (PCA):** PCA reduces the dimensions of the dataset, preserving significant features while simplifying the data.
- **Anomaly Detection Algorithms:** These algorithms are designed to identify unusual patterns or data points, commonly applied in fraud detection and system monitoring.

Neural Networks and Backpropagation
Neural networks are a subset of machine learning models inspired by the human brain. They consist of layers of nodes, or "neurons," connected by weights that adjust as the network learns from data. Neural networks are highly effective in handling complex tasks such as image recognition, natural language processing, and deep learning.

Backpropagation:
Backpropagation is a critical process in training neural networks, where errors from the model's predictions are propagated backward to adjust the weights, reducing error over time. This iterative process, combined with optimization techniques like gradient descent, allows neural networks to learn and improve. In essence, backpropagation enables the network to minimize its error rate, improving its predictive accuracy with each iteration.

Fundamentals of Deep Learning

Deep learning represents a significant advancement in artificial intelligence, particularly in the field of machine learning. It focuses on leveraging neural networks to recognize patterns, extract features, and make predictions based on large datasets. Deep learning has become central to applications requiring high-level data processing, like image recognition, natural language processing, and even real-time decision-making.

Neural Network Architectures

In deep learning, **neural networks** are the foundational structures that enable machines to simulate complex human-like tasks. Inspired by the structure of the human brain, neural networks consist of interconnected nodes, known as neurons, arranged in layers. Each neuron performs calculations based on the input it receives, passing the results to other neurons in subsequent layers. Neural networks are typically organized in three types of layers:

1. **Input Layer**: The layer that receives the raw data, like an image or text. Each neuron here represents an individual input feature.
2. **Hidden Layers**: The layers that process and transform the data. These hidden layers contain multiple neurons that adjust their weights based on the learning process, refining the output with each pass. Deep learning networks have multiple hidden layers, allowing for deeper, more intricate feature extraction.
3. **Output Layer**: The final layer that provides the prediction or classification, such as identifying an image as a "cat" or "dog."

The number and structure of hidden layers make a network "deep." Adding layers increases a network's ability to capture complex patterns but also requires more computational power and training data to optimize performance.

Convolution and Convolutional Neural Networks (CNN)

One of the most powerful architectures in deep learning is the **Convolutional Neural Network (CNN)**, especially effective for visual data analysis like image and video recognition. CNNs leverage a mathematical operation called **convolution** to filter and analyze data, extracting critical spatial features (e.g., edges, textures, or shapes) that are crucial for image processing.

1. **Convolutional Layers**: These layers apply a set of small filters, or kernels, that slide across the input image. Each filter detects specific features in the data, such as edges, by performing element-wise multiplication with sections of the input and summing the results. The outcome is a feature map, a processed version of the input image emphasizing the detected features.

2. **Pooling Layers**: Pooling is a technique used to reduce the spatial dimensions of the data, making the network more computationally efficient while retaining important features. The most common type is **max pooling**, where the largest value in a selected region is retained, compressing data without sacrificing essential information.
3. **Fully Connected Layers**: These layers appear toward the end of the network, where each neuron is connected to all neurons in the preceding layer. The fully connected layers aggregate and interpret the features extracted in the convolutional layers, producing the final classification.

CNNs have transformed fields like computer vision due to their ability to handle complex image data and generalize well to new images. By using a hierarchical approach, CNNs start by detecting simple patterns and progressively build towards more complex shapes and objects, making them remarkably efficient at recognizing faces, objects, and even emotions in images.

Programming Languages and Platforms for AI

As the field of Artificial Intelligence (AI) advances, the tools used to develop AI applications have become essential in enabling innovation and deployment. From programming languages to specialized cloud platforms, these resources form the backbone of modern AI systems, providing researchers and developers with the capacity to build, train, and deploy complex models efficiently. This section provides a detailed overview of the main programming language in AI, Python, its key libraries, and the leading AI and cloud platforms that support the field.

Python and its Key Libraries (TensorFlow, PyTorch, Scikit-Learn)

Python has established itself as the dominant programming language in AI due to its readability, versatility, and extensive library ecosystem. With simple syntax and robust support for complex operations, Python is well-suited for both beginners and advanced AI practitioners. The libraries TensorFlow, PyTorch, and Scikit-Learn are among the most popular for AI development, each catering to specific needs within the AI pipeline:

- **TensorFlow**: Developed by Google Brain, TensorFlow is an open-source library specifically designed for deep learning and neural network tasks. It provides flexible tools for building models and offers compatibility with both CPUs and GPUs, making it highly efficient for large-scale data processing. TensorFlow's ecosystem includes TensorBoard for visualizing model performance and TensorFlow Extended (TFX) for deploying models at scale, making it an end-to-end tool for complex AI projects.

- **PyTorch**: Created by Facebook's AI Research lab, PyTorch is a highly popular library known for its dynamic computational graph and intuitive debugging capabilities, making it particularly favored in research and prototyping. It offers a robust set of tools for constructing and training neural networks, and its modular design allows developers to experiment quickly. PyTorch's recent support for mobile deployment (TorchScript) also facilitates the implementation of AI applications in mobile environments.

- **Scikit-Learn**: While TensorFlow and PyTorch are focused on deep learning, Scikit-Learn excels in classical machine learning techniques, such as linear regression, classification, clustering, and dimensionality reduction. Built on top of other Python libraries like NumPy, Scipy, and Matplotlib, Scikit-Learn provides an accessible interface for basic machine learning workflows. It is a go-to library for projects that do not require deep neural networks and is well-suited for rapid data analysis and model prototyping.

Together, these libraries provide the essential tools for building and optimizing AI models, each contributing unique functionalities tailored to the diverse demands of AI projects.

Overview of Major AI and Cloud Platforms (Google AI, AWS, Azure AI)

Cloud platforms have revolutionized the AI field by offering scalable and efficient resources that support model training, data storage, and deployment without requiring extensive local infrastructure. The following platforms are leading in the field of AI, each offering a suite of tools that allow companies and developers to harness the power of AI:

- **Google AI and Google Cloud Platform (GCP)**: Google offers an extensive suite of AI tools, including pre-trained models and customizable machine learning APIs. GCP's AI Hub provides access to TensorFlow Extended, AutoML for creating custom ML models with minimal programming, and BigQuery ML for training models directly on SQL data. Google's infrastructure supports powerful compute resources such as TPUs (Tensor Processing Units), specially optimized for deep learning tasks, making it ideal for data-intensive applications.

- **Amazon Web Services (AWS) AI**: AWS provides a comprehensive range of AI services, including Amazon SageMaker, a powerful platform for building, training, and deploying machine learning models. AWS also offers pre-built AI models for specific applications like text analysis, translation, and image recognition. With its extensive storage and compute options, AWS allows users to scale AI operations based on demand, and services like SageMaker Studio provide an integrated environment for streamlined model management.

- **Microsoft Azure AI**: Azure's AI offerings cover a wide range of machine learning tools, including Azure Machine Learning, which provides a collaborative environment for data scientists to build and deploy models. Azure Cognitive Services offer pre-built APIs for speech, language, and vision processing, allowing developers to integrate these capabilities with minimal effort. Azure's integration with Microsoft's ecosystem also makes it a valuable choice for enterprises already using Microsoft tools, offering scalability and flexibility across diverse AI applications.

These platforms make AI more accessible by offering both infrastructure and specialized tools for development, catering to the needs of organizations from startups to large enterprises.

Pipeline of an AI Project

An AI project pipeline is a structured process involving multiple stages, each critical for transforming raw data into an effective, functional AI model. This pipeline serves as a roadmap for data scientists and engineers to ensure that each step is performed systematically, leading to high-quality, reliable results. This section will walk you through each phase of the AI project pipeline, from gathering raw data to deploying a functioning model, highlighting the importance of careful data preparation along the way.

Steps to Develop an AI Project: From Raw Data to Functional Models
1. **Problem Definition and Goal Setting**
    o **Objective Clarity**: Every AI project begins with a clear understanding of the problem it aims to solve. Defining the goal is essential, as it shapes the direction of the entire project.
    o **Success Metrics**: Establish specific metrics to evaluate the model's performance. Metrics such as accuracy, precision, recall, or mean squared error (MSE) guide whether the AI model meets the required standards.
2. **Data Collection**
    o **Data Sources**: Identify relevant data sources— whether structured databases, external APIs, or web scraping. Data quality and relevance are paramount, as they directly impact the model's outcome.
    o **Data Types**: Collect diverse data types depending on the application. Structured data (tables, databases) and unstructured data (text, images, audio) each require specific handling methods.

3. **Data Cleaning and Preprocessing**
   - **Data Quality Assessment**: Raw data is often incomplete, noisy, or inconsistent. Assessing quality is critical to avoid introducing bias or inaccuracies in the model.
   - **Data Cleaning Steps**: This process includes handling missing values, removing duplicates, and correcting inconsistencies. Techniques such as data imputation and normalization are commonly applied.
   - **Data Transformation**: Converting raw data into a format suitable for machine learning models, often through encoding categorical data, scaling numerical features, or even dimensionality reduction.
4. **Exploratory Data Analysis (EDA)**
   - **Insights Extraction**: EDA is used to understand data patterns, distributions, and relationships. Visualizations (like histograms, scatter plots, and heatmaps) reveal insights that guide feature engineering.
   - **Feature Selection and Engineering**: Identify and create relevant features. Techniques like feature scaling, extraction, and selection help refine the dataset for optimal model performance.
5. **Model Selection**
   - **Choosing the Right Model**: Based on the problem type (classification, regression, clustering), select an appropriate algorithm. For instance, linear regression may be suitable for a regression problem, while convolutional neural networks (CNNs) work well for image processing.
   - **Hyperparameter Tuning**: Optimize model parameters to enhance performance, using techniques like grid search or random search.
6. **Model Training and Evaluation**
   - **Model Training**: The selected model is trained using the prepared data. The model learns patterns by minimizing the error between predictions and actual outcomes.

- **Model Evaluation**: Test the model using evaluation metrics aligned with the project's goals. Common metrics include F1-score for classification or Root Mean Squared Error (RMSE) for regression tasks.
- **Model Iteration**: Often, several iterations are required, refining the model based on performance insights, adjusting parameters, or even reselecting features.

7. **Model Deployment**
   - **Integration into Production**: Once optimized, the model is integrated into a production environment where it can deliver real-time or batch predictions.
   - **Monitoring and Maintenance**: Post-deployment, the model requires monitoring to ensure sustained performance. Periodic updates and re-training with fresh data may be necessary to prevent model drift.

Importance of Data Collection and Cleaning

Data collection and cleaning are foundational steps in any AI project. High-quality data is the cornerstone of a successful AI model, as it determines the model's accuracy, fairness, and generalizability.

- **Data Collection**: Gathering comprehensive, diverse, and relevant data ensures that the model can learn effectively. Poor-quality or biased data leads to flawed models, reinforcing existing biases or failing to generalize across different data samples.
- **Data Cleaning**: Raw data often contains noise or outliers, which can mislead the model if not properly handled. Cleaning the data by addressing missing values, standardizing formats, and ensuring consistency minimizes errors and enhances the model's ability to learn accurately. This step is not just a preliminary task but a fundamental process that sets the stage for every following phase in the AI pipeline.

Goal: Demonstrate a simple supervised Machine Learning model (linear regression) and a basic Deep Learning model (using

TensorFlow). These examples show core technical concepts and common tools.

ML Example (Linear Regression):

```python
from sklearn.linear_model import LinearRegression
import numpy as np

# Synthetic data: y = 2x + 3 + some noise
X = np.array([[i] for i in range(10)])
y = np.array([2*i + 3 + np.random.randn()*0.5 for i in range(10)])

model = LinearRegression()
model.fit(X, y)

print("Coefficient:", model.coef_)
print("Intercept:", model.intercept_)
```

DL Example (Simple Neural Network with TensorFlow):

```python
import tensorflow as tf
import numpy as np

# A simple sequential model with one dense layer
model = tf.keras.Sequential([
    tf.keras.layers.Dense(1, input_shape=(1,))
])

model.compile(optimizer='adam', loss='mse')

# Data: y = 2x + 1
X = np.array([i for i in range(10)], dtype=float)
Y = np.array([2*i + 1 for i in range(10)], dtype=float)

model.fit(X, Y, epochs=100, verbose=0)

print("Prediction for x=10:", model.predict([10.0]))
```

Chapter 4
Applications of AI in the Real World

Applications of AI in the Real World

Artificial Intelligence (AI) has rapidly become a cornerstone of modern society, seamlessly blending into our daily routines and transforming how we interact with technology, consume information, and manage our lives. Although it might seem like a futuristic concept, AI has quietly infiltrated many aspects of our everyday experience, creating conveniences we often take for granted. This chapter delves into some of the most impactful applications of AI in daily life, focusing on virtual assistants, social media, and search engines.

AI in Daily Life

From personalized recommendations on our phones to automated customer service, AI plays a major role in shaping the digital landscape we navigate daily. These AI applications enhance user experience by adapting to individual behaviors, responding to preferences, and even predicting our needs. The following sections examine the specific contributions of virtual assistants, social media algorithms, and search engines to our everyday interactions.

Virtual Assistants

Virtual assistants like Siri, Alexa, and Google Assistant have become household names, reflecting the growing role AI plays in simplifying routine tasks. These assistants leverage powerful algorithms and advanced Natural Language Processing (NLP) to interpret and respond to user commands. NLP enables virtual assistants to "understand" and process human language, allowing them to interact naturally with users.

- **Task Management**: Virtual assistants help with managing day-to-day activities like setting alarms, creating reminders, and scheduling appointments. They can even place calls, send messages, and provide traffic or weather updates.
- **Home Automation**: Integrated with smart home devices, virtual assistants allow users to control lights, thermostats, and security systems through simple voice commands.

- **Information Retrieval**: These assistants are mini search engines at our fingertips. They can quickly access vast databases of knowledge, providing users with quick answers to questions on a wide range of topics, from trivia to complex research.

Over time, virtual assistants learn individual user preferences, making their suggestions and interactions increasingly relevant. The relationship we develop with these virtual assistants is a testament to the power of AI, blending practicality with personal convenience.

Social Media

Social media platforms use AI extensively to create personalized and engaging experiences for their users. Algorithms analyze massive amounts of data in real-time, allowing platforms like Facebook, Instagram, and Twitter to curate content that matches individual interests and behaviors.

- **Content Curation**: Social media algorithms prioritize content based on user interactions like likes, shares, and comments, ensuring that users see posts most relevant to them. This creates a highly personalized news feed tailored to each user's preferences.
- **Image and Video Recognition**: AI-driven image and video recognition technology enables features like auto-tagging friends in photos, suggesting filters, and even flagging potentially inappropriate content for review.
- **Customer Support with Chatbots**: Many social platforms employ AI-driven chatbots to handle customer service queries. These chatbots provide quick responses to common questions, enhancing the user experience and alleviating demand on human support teams.

AI's role in social media is complex, going beyond mere convenience to deeply influence how people interact, engage with content, and perceive the world around them.

Search Engines

Search engines like Google and Bing are prime examples of AI in action, delivering highly relevant and personalized search results within seconds. The efficiency of these platforms lies in their powerful AI algorithms, which process vast quantities of data to rank and retrieve information based on a user's unique query.

- **Ranking Algorithms**: AI-driven ranking algorithms determine which web pages appear at the top of search results. These algorithms consider factors like relevance, content quality, and user history, ensuring that search results are as accurate and useful as possible.
- **Natural Language Processing and Contextual Understanding**: AI enables search engines to comprehend the intent behind queries, even those that are vague or phrased conversationally. This is especially useful in providing answers to complex or ambiguous questions.
- **Personalized Results**: Search engines tailor their results based on user history and preferences, delivering an experience that feels uniquely relevant to each individual.

AI-powered search engines have redefined how we access information, making it quicker, more accurate, and customized to our specific interests.

AI in Industry

Artificial Intelligence has brought transformative changes across various industries, enabling smarter processes, faster decision-making, and personalized services. By leveraging vast data and sophisticated algorithms, AI helps industries achieve higher efficiency, reduce costs, and deliver enhanced user experiences. In this section, we explore AI applications in several critical sectors, including healthcare, finance, automotive, retail and e-commerce, and manufacturing.

Healthcare: Assisted Diagnosis and Personalized Medicine
In healthcare, AI is helping revolutionize diagnostics and treatment plans. Through data analysis and machine learning, AI systems can analyze complex medical data, assisting healthcare professionals in identifying diseases more accurately and creating personalized treatment plans.

- **Assisted Diagnosis**: AI algorithms can process medical images (such as X-rays and MRIs) to detect conditions like tumors, fractures, and infections with a high degree of accuracy. Machine learning models trained on large datasets can detect abnormalities and provide risk assessments, supporting doctors in making informed diagnostic decisions.
- **Personalized Medicine**: AI allows for the customization of treatments based on an individual's unique genetic makeup, lifestyle, and health history. By analyzing patient data, AI can predict which treatments will be most effective, optimizing outcomes while reducing side effects. This personalized approach enhances precision medicine, improving treatment efficacy and patient satisfaction.

AI's contributions to healthcare are life-changing, allowing earlier disease detection, streamlined treatment, and improved patient care.

Finance: Risk Management and Algorithmic Trading
The finance industry relies heavily on AI for both security and strategy. From fraud detection to algorithmic trading, AI helps financial institutions safeguard assets, predict market trends, and make data-driven investment decisions.

- **Risk Management**: AI algorithms analyze vast datasets to detect patterns associated with fraud or credit risks, enabling early intervention. These algorithms can assess risk factors like transaction behavior, financial history, and market fluctuations to help financial institutions make safer lending and investment decisions.
- **Algorithmic Trading**: AI-powered algorithms execute trades at speeds and efficiencies far beyond human capability. By analyzing market conditions in real time, these algorithms capitalize on price changes and execute high-frequency trading strategies, maximizing returns and minimizing risks.

AI's predictive capabilities have strengthened the finance industry, offering tools that enhance security and provide smarter investment solutions.

Automotive: Autonomous Driving and Driver Assistance

In the automotive sector, AI has been pivotal in advancing both autonomous driving technology and driver-assistance systems. From self-driving cars to intelligent safety features, AI is transforming how vehicles operate and interact with drivers.

- **Autonomous Driving**: Self-driving cars rely on a combination of machine learning, computer vision, and sensor technology to navigate roads safely. AI algorithms process data from cameras, radar, and lidar to detect objects, recognize road signs, and make real-time decisions, enabling vehicles to drive autonomously.
- **Driver Assistance**: AI-powered driver-assistance systems, such as lane-keeping, automatic braking, and adaptive cruise control, help prevent accidents by enhancing driver awareness and response times. These systems interpret data from sensors to provide timely feedback or take corrective actions, making driving safer for everyone on the road.

AI's applications in automotive technology represent a leap toward a future of safer, more efficient transportation.

Retail and e-Commerce: Recommendations and Customer Personalization
In the retail and e-commerce industries, AI helps businesses understand customer preferences, providing personalized shopping experiences and efficient product recommendations. By analyzing consumer behavior, AI enables a more targeted approach to marketing and customer service.

- **Recommendations**: AI recommendation engines analyze purchase history, browsing habits, and demographic information to suggest products relevant to individual consumers. This technology improves customer engagement and conversion rates by showing customers products that match their interests.
- **Customer Personalization**: Through machine learning algorithms, businesses can tailor marketing campaigns, promotions, and user interfaces to match each customer's preferences. AI-driven chatbots also enhance customer service by providing instant responses, personalizing interactions, and assisting with inquiries in real time.

The personalized experiences enabled by AI in retail and e-commerce increase customer satisfaction, drive loyalty, and boost sales.

Manufacturing: Predictive Maintenance and Automation
AI plays a crucial role in modern manufacturing by optimizing processes, minimizing downtime, and improving productivity. Through predictive maintenance and automation, AI is reshaping manufacturing operations with cost-effective and efficient solutions.

- **Predictive Maintenance**: AI-powered sensors and analytics monitor machinery health, predicting potential failures before they occur. By analyzing performance data, AI algorithms can identify early warning signs of equipment degradation, allowing for timely maintenance that prevents costly unplanned downtime.
- **Automation**: AI enables automated production lines, optimizing workflows and reducing human error. Robotics powered by AI perform repetitive tasks accurately and efficiently, freeing human workers to focus on complex, value-added activities. This not only enhances productivity but also ensures higher quality and consistency in production.

The integration of AI in manufacturing creates a more resilient and responsive industry, ready to meet the demands of the future.

AI and Creativity

Artificial Intelligence (AI) has opened up a new realm in creative fields, influencing how content is generated and reshaping traditional artistic processes. No longer confined to analytical or repetitive tasks, AI now serves as a co-creator, enabling innovative forms of art, music, and media production. This chapter explores how AI impacts creativity, focusing on automated content generation, including text, images, and music, as well as AI's role in cinematic and artistic production.

Automatic Content Generation (Text, Images, Music)
AI's capability to generate content autonomously has made it an invaluable tool for creatives, providing fresh ideas and accelerating

production processes. Leveraging advanced algorithms, deep learning models, and vast datasets, AI can create compelling text, visually stunning images, and original musical compositions with minimal human intervention.

- **Text Generation**: Natural Language Processing (NLP) enables AI to produce human-like text. This technology powers tools that generate articles, product descriptions, and even poetry. Through sophisticated language models like GPT, AI can mimic specific writing styles or adapt to brand voices, streamlining content creation for marketing, publishing, and journalism.
- **Image Generation**: Generative Adversarial Networks (GANs) are a popular AI tool for creating original images. By training on extensive datasets, GANs learn to generate artwork, product images, and even hyper-realistic portraits. AI-generated images are widely used in marketing, digital art, and virtual reality, expanding the boundaries of what's visually possible.
- **Music Composition**: AI-driven tools like OpenAI's MuseNet or Google's Magenta can compose music across various genres, from classical to jazz and pop. These algorithms analyze patterns in vast music libraries, identifying harmonies, rhythms, and structures to create original compositions. AI-generated music is now found in video games, advertising, and film scores, often complementing human composers by providing fresh creative directions.

The potential for AI in automatic content generation highlights its ability to operate as both a tool and a creative partner, adapting to the nuances of human preferences while introducing unique, often unexpected, creative elements.

AI in Cinematic and Artistic Production

AI's presence in film and art has introduced new approaches to storytelling, visual effects, and artistic expression. By supporting complex creative tasks, AI enhances production quality, efficiency, and artistic vision, enabling creators to push the limits of their work.

- **Film Production**: In the film industry, AI assists in scriptwriting, video editing, and even casting. By analyzing audience data, AI can predict popular plot elements, suggest scene edits, and even create digital actors. For instance, AI-generated characters or "digital doubles" can seamlessly fill in for actors in complex action scenes or allow for realistic de-aging effects.

- **Visual Effects**: AI's role in visual effects (VFX) has grown, automating tasks like scene rendering, object tracking, and special effects generation. Machine learning models can analyze and recreate complex motions, enabling seamless integration of CGI with live-action scenes. This technology drastically reduces time and cost, allowing for more ambitious visual storytelling.
- **Interactive Art Installations**: AI is now an active participant in the art world, creating interactive installations that respond to audience presence or emotional cues. By blending technology with creativity, artists are developing immersive experiences that engage viewers on new sensory and emotional levels.

Through these applications, AI is not merely a tool but a collaborator in the creative process, enabling artists and filmmakers to explore boundaries beyond conventional techniques. Its adaptive capabilities allow for a new level of interactivity and personalization, shaping the future of creative expression.

Goal: Illustrate loading a pre-trained image classification model (Computer Vision) using PyTorch. We show how to preprocess an image and predict its class.

Example (Computer Vision with PyTorch):

```python
import torch
from torchvision import models, transforms
from PIL import Image

# Load a pre-trained ResNet18 model
model = models.resnet18(pretrained=True)
model.eval()

preprocess = transforms.Compose([
    transforms.Resize(224),
    transforms.CenterCrop(224),
    transforms.ToTensor()
])

img = Image.open("cat.jpg")  # Example image
img_t = preprocess(img).unsqueeze(0)

with torch.no_grad():
    outputs = model(img_t)
_, predicted = outputs.max(1)
print("Predicted class index:", predicted.item())
```

Chapter 5
Ethics and Considerations in AI

Ethics and Considerations in AI

As Artificial Intelligence (AI) grows in influence and application, ethical questions and challenges surrounding its use are becoming critical points of discussion. AI offers tremendous potential for positive impact, but it also raises concerns related to fairness, privacy, and security. Addressing these ethical dimensions is essential to ensure that AI technology is used responsibly and equitably. This chapter explores the primary risks and challenges associated with AI, including algorithmic bias, security threats, data privacy, and the ethical management of personal data.

Risks and Challenges of AI

While AI technologies offer numerous benefits, they also present complex challenges. The rapid advancement of AI systems has outpaced the establishment of clear ethical guidelines, leading to potential risks, particularly in the areas of algorithmic bias and security.

Algorithmic Bias and Discrimination

Algorithmic bias is one of the most pressing ethical challenges in AI. AI systems are often trained on vast datasets that may unintentionally reflect societal biases. When AI models learn from these biased datasets, they can perpetuate or even amplify existing inequalities. For instance, facial recognition software has been shown to have higher error rates in recognizing individuals with darker skin tones, leading to potential cases of misidentification.

- **Source of Bias**: Bias in AI can arise from biased data, lack of diversity in training datasets, or the subjective decisions made by developers during the design process.
- **Impact on Society**: Algorithmic bias can lead to discrimination in critical areas like hiring, law enforcement, and lending. For example, a biased hiring algorithm might

inadvertently favor one demographic over another, resulting in an unfair hiring process.
- **Mitigation Strategies**: Ensuring diverse and representative datasets, implementing bias-detection tools, and regularly auditing AI systems can help reduce the risk of discrimination in AI applications.

AI bias remains a critical area of concern, as these systems are increasingly used in decision-making processes that directly impact individuals and communities.

AI Security and Potential Threats

AI security is another major challenge, especially as AI systems become more autonomous and capable of decision-making. The misuse of AI technology poses threats to both individuals and society, including cyberattacks and misinformation.
- **Cybersecurity Risks**: AI systems, especially those connected to the internet, are vulnerable to hacking and manipulation. Malicious actors can exploit weaknesses in AI algorithms, leading to potential data breaches, identity theft, and financial fraud.
- **Autonomous Threats**: With the rise of autonomous systems, such as self-driving cars and drones, there is a risk that these technologies could be used in ways that endanger public safety.
- **Deepfakes and Misinformation**: AI-driven deepfake technology allows the creation of highly realistic but false content, which can be used to spread misinformation, deceive the public, and compromise individuals' reputations.

Addressing security risks in AI requires proactive measures, including the development of robust cybersecurity protocols and regulatory frameworks to prevent misuse.

Privacy and Data Security

With AI systems increasingly relying on personal data, concerns about privacy and data protection have escalated. Safeguarding personal information is essential to maintain public trust and prevent abuse.

Protection of Personal Data

AI systems often rely on large datasets, which can include sensitive personal information. This dependency raises concerns about how personal data is collected, stored, and used.

- **Data Collection**: AI applications often require vast amounts of data to function effectively. However, indiscriminate data collection without user consent can infringe on individual privacy rights.
- **Anonymization and Encryption**: Implementing data anonymization and encryption techniques can help protect individual identities while still allowing AI systems to leverage useful information.
- **User Consent**: Providing users with control over their personal data, including options to consent to or withdraw from data collection, is crucial for ethical AI development.

Effective data protection policies help create transparency and trust between AI developers and users, promoting a more secure AI environment.

Ethical and Legal Data Management

The ethical management of data goes beyond technical solutions and includes legal considerations to ensure that AI development respects individual rights and societal values.

- **Regulations and Compliance**: Legal frameworks, such as the General Data Protection Regulation (GDPR) in Europe, establish guidelines for ethical data use and require companies to implement data protection measures.
- **Transparency**: AI developers and companies are encouraged to maintain transparency about data usage, allowing individuals to understand how their information is utilized.
- **Accountability**: Establishing accountability mechanisms ensures that companies are responsible for any misuse or mishandling of data.

Ethical and legal data management is essential to prevent exploitation, discrimination, and misuse of information, fostering a fair and responsible AI ecosystem.

Applications of AI in the Real World

The impact of Artificial Intelligence (AI) extends beyond personal convenience and digital engagement; it is fundamentally reshaping the workforce and challenging existing regulatory frameworks. This chapter examines two significant areas where AI's influence is profound and complex: employment and regulation. As AI technologies evolve, they create both opportunities and challenges, necessitating a shift in skills for the workforce and prompting governments worldwide to consider regulations to ensure AI's ethical and fair development.

AI and Employment

The adoption of AI across various industries has sparked widespread debate about its impact on employment. While AI enables automation of repetitive tasks and increases efficiency, it also raises concerns about job displacement. Simultaneously, AI creates a demand for new skills, prompting workers to adapt and upskill. Here, we explore both the challenges and opportunities AI brings to the workforce.

Impact of AI on Employment

AI's ability to automate routine tasks has led to significant changes in sectors like manufacturing, retail, and customer service. Repetitive and predictable tasks, such as data entry or simple assembly line work, are increasingly handled by AI-driven machines, improving productivity and reducing costs. However, this shift has led to concerns about job displacement, particularly in roles requiring minimal specialization.

- **Job Displacement**: As AI takes over routine tasks, certain job categories, particularly those based on repetitive processes, are at risk of being eliminated or reduced. However, this trend also varies by sector, with industries such as healthcare and education less impacted due to the need for human interaction and expertise.
- **Job Transformation**: Rather than completely replacing jobs, AI is transforming them. For instance, in customer service, AI chatbots handle simple inquiries, freeing human agents to focus on complex issues requiring empathy and problem-solving skills.
- **Emergence of New Roles**: The development of AI and machine learning has led to the creation of new job roles, including data scientists, AI ethics specialists, and machine learning engineers. These roles focus on developing, maintaining, and monitoring AI systems, requiring specialized technical knowledge.

The AI-driven workforce transformation highlights the importance of adaptability. Workers will need to embrace new skills and adjust to shifting job functions as automation continues to shape the employment landscape.

New Skills and Preparing for the Future

As AI reshapes the job market, there is a growing demand for digital skills and specialized knowledge. Workers are increasingly required to develop competencies that complement AI systems, such as data analysis, critical thinking, and problem-solving.

- **Digital Literacy**: Familiarity with AI concepts, such as data analysis and machine learning, has become essential in many industries. Organizations are investing in training programs to equip employees with foundational knowledge in these areas.
- **Soft Skills**: Skills like critical thinking, creativity, and emotional intelligence remain valuable as they are challenging to automate. For instance, healthcare providers

and educators rely heavily on these interpersonal skills, ensuring their relevance in the AI-driven workforce.

- **Lifelong Learning**: Continuous education is key. As AI technologies evolve, the workforce must stay current with advancements. Programs like online courses, certifications, and vocational training have become popular avenues for workers looking to upskill.

AI is not just changing what skills are necessary but also fostering a culture of lifelong learning and adaptability, essential traits for future job stability.

AI and Regulation

As AI becomes more integrated into society, regulatory frameworks must adapt to ensure ethical, transparent, and responsible use of these technologies. While AI offers numerous benefits, it also raises questions about data privacy, accountability, and fairness. Here, we examine existing regulations and potential future frameworks that could shape the development and deployment of AI.

International and Local Regulations on AI

Several countries have begun to establish guidelines and policies governing the use of AI, recognizing the need to protect individual rights and promote transparency. International organizations such as the European Union (EU) and the Organisation for Economic Co-operation and Development (OECD) are at the forefront of creating frameworks that encourage responsible AI development.

- **The EU's General Data Protection Regulation (GDPR)**: The GDPR is a landmark regulation in data privacy, which impacts AI systems handling personal data. It mandates transparency, data minimization, and accountability, requiring organizations to explain AI decisions that affect individuals.
- **The OECD AI Principles**: Adopted by 42 countries, these principles emphasize human-centered AI, transparency, and accountability. They guide nations in promoting ethical AI practices that respect privacy and human rights.

- **Local Efforts**: Some countries, like the United States, have taken a sector-specific approach, regulating AI in sensitive areas like healthcare and finance, where data privacy and ethical use are particularly critical.

These regulations reflect a growing consensus on the need for oversight, though approaches vary across regions based on cultural and societal values.

Perspectives for AI Regulation

Looking ahead, the regulatory landscape for AI is likely to become more comprehensive as AI technology continues to advance. Policymakers and stakeholders are discussing frameworks to address issues such as bias, transparency, and accountability.

- **Ethical AI and Bias Prevention**: One significant focus is on ensuring AI systems are free from bias. Regulations may require companies to audit algorithms regularly to prevent discriminatory practices in areas like hiring or lending.
- **Transparency and Explainability**: There is a push for regulations mandating that AI systems be explainable, allowing users and regulators to understand how decisions are made. This is especially relevant in sectors like finance and criminal justice, where decisions have significant personal impacts.
- **Global Cooperation**: AI is a global phenomenon, necessitating international cooperation to establish unified standards and protocols. Organizations are working to create frameworks that transcend borders, allowing for safe, ethical AI practices worldwide.

The future of AI regulation aims to balance innovation with the protection of individual rights, ensuring that AI serves society in a responsible and ethical manner.

Goal: Show a basic example of checking dataset distribution to detect potential class imbalance—a simple proxy for identifying bias issues.

Example (Checking for Bias):

```python
# Example dataset labels: 0=class1, 1=class2
labels = [0,0,0,1,1,0,1,1,0,0,1,1,1]
count_0 = labels.count(0)
count_1 = labels.count(1)

print("Count class 0:", count_0)
print("Count class 1:", count_1)

if abs(count_0 - count_1) > len(labels)*0.3:
    print("Warning: Potential class imbalance detected.")
```

Chapter 6
Getting Started with Artificial Intelligence

Getting Started with Artificial Intelligence

The journey into Artificial Intelligence (AI) can seem daunting, especially with its technical depth and the vast array of resources available. However, with structured learning paths, accessible resources, and vibrant online communities, beginners can build a solid foundation in AI and progressively advance to more complex topics. This chapter provides guidance on resources for AI learning, including recommended online courses, tutorials, books, and communities where learners can connect, share knowledge, and gain practical insights from experts.

Resources for Learning AI

Learning AI requires dedication, curiosity, and a structured approach. While AI is a complex field, it's accessible to anyone willing to invest time and effort. Below are some key resources to help beginners get started, offering both foundational knowledge and specialized insights to enhance understanding.

Online Courses, Tutorials, and Recommended Books

The availability of high-quality online courses has made AI education more accessible than ever. Renowned institutions and educational platforms offer courses ranging from beginner to advanced levels, allowing learners to build expertise at their own pace. Here's a look at some popular resources:

- **Online Courses**: Platforms like Coursera, edX, Udacity, and DataCamp offer structured courses on AI fundamentals, often developed by prestigious universities and companies. Courses like Andrew Ng's "Machine Learning" on Coursera provide an excellent foundation, covering the basics of algorithms, data handling, and AI applications. Additionally, Udacity's "Artificial Intelligence Nanodegree" delves deeper into topics such as neural networks, computer vision, and natural language processing.
- **Tutorials and Hands-On Practice**: For practical learning, platforms like Kaggle and GitHub host AI tutorials, datasets, and code repositories. Kaggle, in particular, provides free "Kaggle Learn" courses, which are great for beginners to start coding with Python, explore machine learning basics, and work on real-world data science projects.

- **Books**: For a thorough understanding, books such as "Artificial Intelligence: A Modern Approach" by Stuart Russell and Peter Norvig, and "Deep Learning" by Ian Goodfellow, Yoshua Bengio, and Aaron Courville are invaluable resources. These texts cover the theoretical underpinnings and applications of AI, serving as excellent references as learners progress.

Books, tutorials, and courses each offer unique benefits. Together, they build a comprehensive skill set, combining theoretical foundations with hands-on skills essential for AI development.

Online Communities, Forums, and Blogs

AI's dynamic and collaborative nature has given rise to numerous online communities where learners, researchers, and professionals exchange insights, troubleshoot problems, and discuss emerging trends. Engaging with these communities can accelerate learning and provide valuable networking opportunities.

- **Online Communities and Forums**: Platforms like Reddit (e.g., r/MachineLearning), Stack Overflow, and AI-specific communities on Discord allow learners to ask questions, solve coding issues, and get feedback from more experienced practitioners. Stack Overflow is particularly useful for troubleshooting coding errors, with a wide array of solutions contributed by an active user base.
- **Blogs and Websites**: Websites like Towards Data Science, Medium, and AI-related blogs offer valuable insights, tutorials, and case studies on AI applications. Many blogs provide articles by industry professionals, bridging the gap between academic concepts and practical implementation. Subscribing to blogs or newsletters such as those from OpenAI, DeepMind, and Google AI ensures that learners stay updated on the latest research and advancements.

Engaging with online communities and regularly reading AI-focused content helps learners remain current with industry trends and strengthens their understanding through real-world applications. Networking within these communities also opens doors to mentorship and collaboration, crucial elements in the journey to mastering AI.

Development Tools for Beginners

Starting a journey in Artificial Intelligence (AI) and Machine Learning (ML) can be both exciting and challenging. A key part of the process is understanding and mastering essential tools that facilitate the development of AI models and applications. This chapter focuses on practical development tools specifically aimed at beginners, providing step-by-step guidance on setting up Python and using fundamental libraries, as well as basic projects to kickstart learning through hands-on practice.

Installing Python and Using Core Libraries
Python has emerged as the preferred language for AI and ML development due to its readability, extensive library support, and large community. Installing Python and learning to use its main libraries form the foundation of any AI project. Here's a breakdown of the installation steps and an introduction to some of the core libraries that make Python so powerful for AI.

- **Installing Python**: Beginners should start by downloading Python from the official website (python.org). It's recommended to install the latest version, as it will have the most updated features and library support. Once downloaded, the Python installer walks users through a simple setup process, which includes configuring the PATH variable, ensuring Python can be used from the command line.
- **Using Key Libraries**: Python's power in AI comes largely from its extensive libraries designed for data manipulation, ML, and data visualization. Here are some essential libraries for beginners:
  - **NumPy**: Useful for mathematical and statistical operations, essential for handling arrays and matrices.
  - **Pandas**: Provides data structures like DataFrames, which simplify data manipulation and analysis.
  - **Matplotlib and Seaborn**: These are visualization libraries that help in creating charts, graphs, and other visual insights from data.
  - **Scikit-Learn**: A fundamental library for machine learning, Scikit-Learn includes a wide range of

algorithms for classification, regression, clustering, and more. Its intuitive API is designed for ease of use, making it an excellent choice for beginners.

These tools collectively create a comprehensive setup for initial AI and ML projects, allowing users to perform tasks from data preprocessing to model training and evaluation.

Basic Projects to Get Started (Practical Examples of Simple ML Models)

Once the tools are set up, it's time to get hands-on with ML projects. Beginner-friendly projects provide a controlled environment to learn by doing, allowing users to see the entire process of ML development, from data handling to model evaluation. Below are some simple project ideas to build foundational skills:

1. **House Price Prediction with Linear Regression**

Linear regression is one of the simplest ML algorithms and is ideal for understanding basic model-building processes. Using a dataset with features like square footage, location, and age of the house, beginners can predict house prices. Scikit-Learn provides a streamlined approach to implementing linear regression, which includes dividing the data into training and testing sets, training the model, and evaluating its performance.

2. **Iris Species Classification with k-Nearest Neighbors (k-NN)**

This classic ML problem involves classifying iris flowers into species based on petal and sepal measurements. The k-Nearest Neighbors algorithm, which classifies data based on the nearest "neighbors," is straightforward to implement and interpret. The Iris dataset, readily available in Scikit-Learn, is perfect for practicing data visualization and model building.

3. **Handwritten Digit Recognition with Logistic Regression**

Using the MNIST dataset of handwritten digits, beginners can implement a logistic regression model to recognize numbers from 0 to 9. Although it's a simple classification task, it introduces learners to image data and the basics of data transformation, which are essential skills in computer vision.

These projects offer a step-by-step experience with fundamental ML concepts, helping beginners understand how to structure projects, work with data, and evaluate model performance. Building a solid foundation with these examples opens doors to more advanced AI projects down the line.

Practical Exercises and Mini-Projects

Learning about Artificial Intelligence (AI) and Machine Learning (ML) becomes truly rewarding when concepts are applied in hands-on projects. Practical exercises and mini-projects give learners the chance to implement foundational ML techniques and understand how these models function in real-world scenarios. This section provides a step-by-step guide to simple ML projects, such as prediction and classification, along with ideas for personal projects to deepen understanding and skills.

Step-by-Step Guide to Simple ML Projects (e.g., Prediction, Classification)
Building and training ML models might sound intimidating, but starting with manageable projects can simplify the learning process. Here, we'll break down the steps for creating basic ML projects, focusing on two fundamental applications: prediction and classification.

1. Prediction Project: House Price Prediction
Predictive models are a common use of ML, with applications in finance, healthcare, real estate, and more. A house price prediction model is an excellent beginner project that utilizes regression techniques to forecast values based on historical data.
- **Step 1: Data Collection**
Start by collecting a dataset, such as one from a reliable source like Kaggle. For a house price prediction model, the dataset should include features like square footage, number of bedrooms, location, and age of the property.
- **Step 2: Data Preprocessing**
Clean the data by handling any missing values, normalizing or scaling numerical data, and encoding categorical variables like neighborhood or property type.
- **Step 3: Model Selection**

For this project, a linear regression model is a good starting point as it is simple and effective for continuous data. You can later experiment with more complex models, such as decision trees or random forests.

- **Step 4: Model Training and Evaluation**

Split the dataset into training and testing sets. Train the model on the training data and evaluate its accuracy on the test set using metrics like Mean Squared Error (MSE) to assess the model's performance.

- **Step 5: Fine-Tuning and Deployment**

Experiment with hyperparameter tuning to improve the model's accuracy. Once satisfied, you can use the model to make predictions on new data or deploy it using a web interface for real-time use.

2. Classification Project: Spam Detection

Classification projects are ideal for beginners and have numerous applications, from fraud detection to sentiment analysis. Spam detection, for instance, helps identify unwanted emails and is a practical example of binary classification.

- **Step 1: Data Collection**

Acquire a labeled dataset, where emails are marked as "spam" or "not spam." This can be found in open repositories like UCI Machine Learning Repository.

- **Step 2: Data Preprocessing**

Clean the text data by removing punctuation, converting words to lowercase, and removing stop words. Use techniques like TF-IDF (Term Frequency-Inverse Document Frequency) to transform the text data into numerical form.

- **Step 3: Model Selection**

A Naive Bayes classifier is a good choice for text-based classification tasks due to its efficiency and accuracy on sparse data. More advanced learners might explore support vector machines or neural networks.

- **Step 4: Model Training and Evaluation**

Train the model on the labeled data and test its performance using metrics like accuracy, precision, and recall. This will help you determine how well the model identifies spam emails.

- **Step 5: Model Optimization and Deployment**

Fine-tune the model by adjusting parameters or using different text vectorization techniques. Once ready, the model can be integrated into an email client to filter incoming messages in real-time.

Ideas for Personal Projects to Deepen Understanding
For those interested in further exploring ML, here are a few project ideas that build on prediction and classification techniques and allow for creativity and problem-solving:
- **Sentiment Analysis for Product Reviews**

Build a sentiment analysis model that classifies customer reviews as positive, neutral, or negative. This project involves NLP techniques and is useful for applications in e-commerce and customer service.
- **Image Classification with Convolutional Neural Networks (CNNs)**

Try a project that uses CNNs to classify images. You could work with a dataset of flowers or animals to build a model that identifies different species or categories.
- **Stock Market Price Prediction**

Create a time-series model to predict stock prices based on historical data. This project helps you learn about more advanced topics like time-series analysis and financial forecasting.

These personal projects offer the opportunity to delve deeper into AI and ML, exploring complex techniques and gaining practical experience with real-world data and problems.

Goal: Provide a beginner-friendly example of loading data, training a simple model, and evaluating performance. This introduces the practical steps of an AI project workflow.

Example (Simple Classification with scikit-learn):

```python
import pandas as pd
from sklearn.linear_model import LogisticRegression
from sklearn.model_selection import train_test_split
from sklearn.metrics import accuracy_score

# Assuming features.csv has columns: "feature1", "feature2", "label"
data = pd.read_csv("features.csv")
X = data[["feature1", "feature2"]]
y = data["label"]

X_train, X_test, y_train, y_test = train_test_split(X, y, test_size=0.2)

model = LogisticRegression()
model.fit(X_train, y_train)

predictions = model.predict(X_test)
acc = accuracy_score(y_test, predictions)
print("Accuracy:", acc)
```

Chapter 7

Future Perspectives of Artificial Intelligence

Future Perspectives of Artificial Intelligence

Artificial Intelligence (AI) is advancing at an astonishing pace, with innovations reshaping our understanding of what machines can accomplish and how they can augment human potential. As we look toward the future of AI, certain trends are expected to drive the next wave of development. This chapter examines these emerging trends, focusing on advancements in neural networks, the rise of explainable AI, and the transformative potential of quantum computing in the AI landscape.

Current AI Trends

Today, the field of AI is undergoing rapid advancements, with research efforts concentrated on making AI not only more powerful but also more transparent and understandable. This evolution is crucial to building systems that can gain public trust and be integrated safely across sectors like healthcare, finance, and autonomous driving. Key developments in advanced neural networks and explainable AI (XAI), along with breakthroughs in quantum computing, represent the forefront of AI research.

Progress in Advanced Neural Networks and Explainable AI

The foundation of modern AI lies in neural networks, complex algorithms inspired by the human brain that allow machines to learn from data and make decisions. Recent innovations have led to more sophisticated neural networks, known as "deep neural networks" or "advanced neural networks." These networks possess multiple layers and can process vast amounts of data, making them capable of tackling complex problems like image recognition, natural language understanding, and predictive analytics.

- **Advanced Neural Networks**: Techniques like convolutional neural networks (CNNs) and recurrent neural networks (RNNs) enable specialized processing in domains such as image analysis and language translation. The advent of generative adversarial networks (GANs) has further revolutionized fields like content creation and medical imaging.
- **Explainable AI (XAI)**: As AI systems become more complex, the need for transparency grows. Explainable AI aims to make the decision-making processes of these

complex models more interpretable to humans. XAI tools help reveal how models arrive at certain decisions, providing insights into their logic and identifying potential biases. This transparency is crucial for sectors like healthcare and finance, where understanding the "why" behind AI decisions is essential for ethical and regulatory compliance.

The combination of advanced neural networks and XAI is paving the way for a future where AI systems are not only highly capable but also trustworthy and accountable.

AI in Quantum Computing

Quantum computing, a revolutionary approach to computation based on the principles of quantum mechanics, holds the promise of transforming AI by drastically enhancing processing capabilities. Unlike classical computers, which use binary (0s and 1s) to process data, quantum computers use quantum bits, or qubits, which can represent multiple states simultaneously. This allows for computations that are exponentially faster and more efficient, particularly beneficial for complex AI tasks.

- **Increased Computational Power**: Quantum computing has the potential to exponentially accelerate machine learning algorithms, enabling AI systems to process enormous datasets and solve intricate problems more efficiently. For instance, tasks like optimization and pattern recognition in large datasets, which are computationally demanding on classical computers, could be executed far more rapidly on quantum systems.
- **Enhanced AI Model Training**: Quantum computing could revolutionize how neural networks are trained by significantly reducing the time and resources required for training deep learning models. This would open doors to more sophisticated AI applications, such as real-time predictive analytics and AI models that can dynamically adapt to new data.
- **New AI Capabilities**: Quantum AI could enable capabilities that are currently beyond the reach of classical AI, including more accurate simulations, cryptographic advancements, and improved natural language processing. These advancements

would push the boundaries of AI applications in fields like drug discovery, climate modeling, and cybersecurity. Although quantum computing is still in its early stages, its integration with AI is anticipated to lead to breakthroughs that were previously unimaginable, positioning quantum AI as a game-changer for the industry's future.

Vision for the Future of AI

Artificial Intelligence (AI) is already deeply embedded in the fabric of modern life, but the journey is far from over. The future of AI holds the promise of remarkable advancements, particularly as we move toward Artificial General Intelligence (AGI). Unlike the current AI systems, which are highly specialized, AGI aims to achieve a more human-like intelligence—capable of reasoning, learning, and adapting across diverse tasks with the versatility seen in human cognition. This section explores the potential impacts of AGI on society, examining both optimistic and pessimistic scenarios that could shape the world.

What Could AGI Mean for Society?

AGI, or Artificial General Intelligence, represents a hypothetical form of AI that can perform any intellectual task a human can do. If achieved, AGI would not only process information and learn independently, but it would also be able to comprehend and navigate complex, nuanced concepts. This leap would enable machines to operate autonomously across a variety of domains, potentially outperforming human cognitive abilities in tasks ranging from scientific research to complex decision-making. However, this brings both immense potential and considerable challenges.

1. **Enhanced Problem-Solving Capabilities**: With AGI, we could tackle some of the world's most pressing issues, such as climate change, energy shortages, and complex medical conditions, by employing intelligent systems that can analyze vast datasets, simulate potential solutions, and innovate beyond human capacity.

2. **Automation of Complex Tasks**: AGI could take automation to a new level, handling tasks that currently require human intuition and adaptability, such as high-level management, strategy development, and creative work.

3. **Cognitive Collaboration with Humans**: Rather than replacing human roles, AGI could operate as a collaborative partner, augmenting human intelligence and providing insights that enhance decision-making across multiple industries.

The implications of AGI are immense, from revolutionizing industries to reshaping societal structures. However, the potential risks also merit attention, as AGI could disrupt employment, pose ethical dilemmas, and challenge existing legal frameworks.

Optimistic and Pessimistic Scenarios

The development of AGI offers both exhilarating possibilities and serious risks. Below are two distinct scenarios, one optimistic and the other pessimistic, illustrating potential future outcomes.

Optimistic Scenario

In an optimistic future, AGI functions as a tool for collective progress, elevating humanity and enhancing quality of life:

- **Healthcare Breakthroughs**: AGI could lead to unprecedented advances in healthcare, including cures for diseases, personalized medicine, and enhanced diagnostics. With AGI's capability to process complex medical data, doctors could receive real-time, highly accurate insights, transforming patient outcomes.
- **Environmental Sustainability**: AGI could drive large-scale environmental solutions, from optimizing renewable energy sources to predicting and mitigating the impacts of climate change. With precise data analysis, AGI could help us create sustainable living systems that balance human needs with environmental preservation.
- **Education and Knowledge Access**: AGI could democratize knowledge, providing advanced, personalized education to people worldwide. By adapting to individual learning styles and offering high-quality resources, AGI-powered educational systems could bridge gaps in education and increase access to knowledge.

In this scenario, AGI serves humanity, enhancing quality of life, reducing inequalities, and driving sustainable innovation.

Pessimistic Scenario

Conversely, a pessimistic scenario foresees AGI posing significant risks that could lead to unintended consequences or exacerbate existing issues:

- **Job Displacement and Economic Inequality**: Widespread automation could lead to massive job displacement, especially in roles traditionally requiring human cognition and adaptability. As AGI takes on complex roles, income inequality could worsen, leaving large portions of the workforce struggling to find meaningful employment.
- **Loss of Human Autonomy**: AGI, without proper safeguards, could operate beyond human control, making decisions that prioritize efficiency over human welfare. This could lead to scenarios where AGI systems enforce rules that conflict with individual freedoms or societal values.
- **Ethical and Security Risks**: In a scenario where AGI lacks ethical grounding or is used with malicious intent, the risks could range from data exploitation to security threats. AGI systems might be misused in areas like surveillance, creating privacy concerns and reducing civil liberties.

In this pessimistic view, AGI could lead to social disruption, ethical dilemmas, and risks to personal autonomy, underscoring the importance of ethical frameworks and regulatory oversight.

Conclusion and Final Reflections

As we reach the conclusion of this exploration into Artificial Intelligence, it's important to synthesize the core concepts and reflect on the profound impact AI will have on both individual lives and society at large. This final chapter consolidates our understanding of AI, highlighting its transformative potential and discussing the broad implications that advancements in AI are likely to have on a personal and global scale.

Summary of Key Concepts Covered

Throughout this journey, we have explored the foundational principles and various applications of AI, from its technical underpinnings to its everyday use cases. Let's revisit some of the essential concepts that form the foundation of AI:

- **Definition and Types of AI**: We began by understanding what AI is and the distinction between narrow AI (specialized to perform specific tasks) and general AI (hypothetical systems capable of human-like cognition).

- **Core Technologies**: AI's main components—machine learning, deep learning, natural language processing (NLP), and computer vision—each contribute to the diverse capabilities that make AI a powerful tool.
- **Real-World Applications**: From virtual assistants that help with daily tasks to advanced algorithms that drive social media engagement, AI has become integral to various industries and personal experiences.
- **Ethical Considerations**: With the benefits of AI come ethical challenges. Issues like privacy, bias in AI systems, and potential job displacement demand thoughtful approaches and regulatory oversight to ensure responsible AI use.

This overview provided not only a technical understanding of AI but also a broader appreciation of its capabilities, limitations, and ethical complexities.

How AI Will Change the World: Personal and Global Implications

The future of AI promises a profound transformation that will touch nearly every facet of human life. Let's consider some of the far-reaching ways in which AI might shape the world.

- **Personalized Experiences**: On an individual level, AI is increasingly being tailored to anticipate personal needs, creating more customized interactions across digital platforms, healthcare, and even education. AI-powered tools could transform everything from personal health tracking to learning environments, adapting to each person's unique characteristics and preferences.
- **Workplace Transformation**: AI will likely change how we work by automating repetitive tasks, augmenting human decision-making, and potentially creating new job roles that require advanced analytical and technical skills. However, it may also bring significant shifts in employment as some traditional roles become obsolete.
- **Scientific and Medical Advances**: AI's analytical capabilities have already proven transformative in fields like

genomics, drug discovery, and diagnostics. By accelerating research and refining complex data, AI could lead to breakthroughs in treating diseases, understanding human biology, and extending life expectancy.

- **Environmental and Global Impact**: AI offers tools for addressing global challenges like climate change, energy management, and sustainable agriculture. Machine learning models can analyze environmental data to optimize energy use, manage resources, and even model climate scenarios to inform policy-making.

As AI technology advances, we will face critical questions about the role it should play in society, how to manage its impact responsibly, and how to prepare for a future where AI coexists with humanity. These questions highlight the dual potential of AI to drive both unprecedented growth and equally significant ethical considerations. Ultimately, AI's future depends on our ability to navigate its challenges, harness its capabilities, and direct its development in ways that benefit society as a whole. The coming years will require collaborative effort from technologists, policymakers, and the public to ensure that AI's influence remains positive and enriching for all.

Goal: Introduce the concept of explainable AI (XAI) briefly. This snippet uses SHAP (if installed) to interpret a model's predictions, illustrating the trend toward more transparent AI models.

Example (Explainable AI with SHAP):

```python
# Requires: pip install shap xgboost
import shap
import xgboost
import pandas as pd

X = pd.DataFrame({
    "age": [25, 35, 45, 55],
    "income": [50000, 60000, 70000, 80000]
})
y = [0, 0, 1, 1]

model = xgboost.XGBClassifier().fit(X, y)
explainer = shap.TreeExplainer(model)
shap_values = explainer.shap_values(X)

shap.summary_plot(shap_values, X)
```

Appendices and Additional Resources

To provide a comprehensive foundation, this appendix includes a glossary of essential technical terms frequently encountered in discussions about Artificial Intelligence. Understanding these terms will help beginners navigate the complex landscape of AI, ensuring they can engage with technical discussions, interpret research findings, and explore AI independently.

The following glossary presents clear definitions, with context and examples to make each term more approachable. Rather than simply listing definitions, we aim to bring each term to life, showing how they fit into the bigger picture of AI.

Glossary of Technical Terms

Algorithm

An algorithm is a set of instructions or rules designed to solve a specific problem or perform a computation. In AI, algorithms are used to process data, learn from it, and make predictions or decisions. For example, recommendation systems on streaming platforms use algorithms to suggest movies or music based on past user behavior.

Artificial Neural Network (ANN)

An artificial neural network is a model inspired by the human brain's structure, comprising layers of nodes (neurons) that process information. ANNs are essential in machine learning and are commonly used in tasks like image and speech recognition.

Big Data

Big Data refers to extremely large data sets that cannot be processed using traditional methods due to their volume, variety, and velocity. AI systems use big data to learn patterns and make more accurate predictions. An example includes predictive analytics in healthcare, where large datasets help to identify potential health risks in patients.

Deep Learning

A subset of machine learning, deep learning involves neural networks with multiple layers, or "deep" architectures, enabling machines to process complex patterns. This technique is widely used in image and voice recognition, as well as in autonomous vehicles.

Machine Learning (ML)

Machine learning is the process by which computers learn from data without being explicitly programmed. ML models identify patterns, enabling applications like spam filtering and predictive text.

Natural Language Processing (NLP)

NLP is the field of AI focused on enabling machines to understand and interpret human language. Common NLP applications include chatbots, voice assistants, and language translation services.

Overfitting

Overfitting occurs when an AI model learns the training data too closely, capturing noise or irrelevant details, which can reduce its accuracy on new data. It's a common issue in machine learning and requires techniques like cross-validation to address.

Reinforcement Learning

A type of machine learning where an agent learns by interacting with its environment, receiving rewards or penalties based on its actions. This approach is frequently used in training AI for game playing, robotics, and autonomous driving.

Supervised Learning

In supervised learning, a model is trained using labeled data, meaning each input has a corresponding correct output. This type of learning is common in applications like image classification and fraud detection.

Unsupervised Learning

Unlike supervised learning, unsupervised learning works with unlabeled data, where the model learns patterns without explicit instructions. It's often used in clustering data and anomaly detection.

These terms form the basis of AI vocabulary, giving readers the tools to navigate further research, deepen their understanding, and engage with new advancements in the field.

Appendices and Additional Resources

In the journey to understand Artificial Intelligence, this ebook has covered foundational principles, technical concepts, and real-world applications. However, as a constantly evolving field, AI offers limitless opportunities for deeper exploration. For those who wish to expand their knowledge, this section provides a curated list of recommended resources, including books, online courses, websites, and videos. These materials are carefully chosen to guide both beginners and advanced learners, providing insights into the latest AI advancements, practical applications, and thought-provoking ethical discussions.

Recommended Resources

The field of AI is rich with learning resources, each designed to offer unique perspectives and specialized knowledge. Below is a selection of some of the best resources for continued learning in AI. These materials can serve as tools to reinforce the concepts covered in this ebook or provide advanced insights for those seeking to deepen their understanding.

Books

1. **"Artificial Intelligence: A Modern Approach" by Stuart Russell and Peter Norvig**

Widely regarded as a comprehensive introduction to AI, this book covers both theoretical foundations and practical applications. Suitable for beginners and professionals alike, it provides a well-rounded view of AI, complete with exercises and real-world examples.

2. **"Deep Learning" by Ian Goodfellow, Yoshua Bengio, and Aaron Courville**

This book delves into deep learning, one of AI's most exciting fields. Written by leading experts, it provides in-depth knowledge on neural networks and is an essential resource for those interested in machine learning and complex data analysis.

3. **"Life 3.0: Being Human in the Age of Artificial Intelligence" by Max Tegmark**

This thought-provoking book examines AI's future implications on society, ethics, and humanity's place in an AI-driven world. It's an excellent choice for readers interested in the philosophical and ethical dimensions of AI.

Online Courses

1. **"Machine Learning" by Andrew Ng (Coursera)**

This popular course offers a robust introduction to machine learning concepts and algorithms, taught by one of the field's pioneers. It covers essential AI techniques like supervised learning, unsupervised learning, and deep learning basics.

2. **"Deep Learning Specialization" by Andrew Ng and Deeplearning.ai (Coursera)**

Designed for learners interested in neural networks and deep learning, this course series provides hands-on practice and covers advanced AI techniques, such as convolutional and recurrent neural networks.

3. **"AI for Everyone" by Andrew Ng (Coursera)**

A non-technical course that introduces the fundamentals of AI to a general audience, explaining AI's applications, limitations, and the ethical considerations of its use. This course is ideal for professionals looking to incorporate AI insights into their industry.

Websites

1. **AI News (ai.google)**

Google's dedicated AI blog provides the latest updates in AI research, applications, and industry trends. It's an excellent resource for staying informed about cutting-edge developments.

2. **Towards Data Science (towardsdatascience.com)**

A popular online platform with a wealth of articles, tutorials, and guides on AI and data science. It's a practical resource for learning new skills and reading about recent innovations in AI.

3. **MIT Technology Review (technologyreview.com)**

This website offers insightful articles on AI and other technologies. With a focus on innovation and societal impact, it provides a comprehensive view of how AI is shaping our world.

Videos

1. **"The Artificial Intelligence Channel" (YouTube)**

This channel features lectures and discussions on AI from leading experts, covering a range of topics from machine learning to AI ethics.

2. **"DeepMind: Solving Intelligence" (YouTube)**

DeepMind's YouTube channel showcases the groundbreaking research being conducted in AI, from gaming to real-world problem-solving.

3. **"TED Talks on Artificial Intelligence" (TED.com)**

TED's curated playlist on AI includes inspiring talks that explore the implications, challenges, and future of AI, offering insights from industry leaders and visionaries.

By exploring these resources, readers can expand their understanding, engage with cutting-edge discussions, and cultivate skills that will prepare them for a future where AI continues to shape industries and societies worldwide. This knowledge journey doesn't end here—it's an open invitation to stay curious, explore widely, and consider both the potential and responsibility that come with AI.

Exercises and Quizzes
As we conclude each section, it's essential to reinforce learning through exercises and quizzes that allow readers to test their understanding of key concepts. This final section provides practical exercises and summary quizzes designed to consolidate knowledge, encourage deeper engagement, and highlight areas for further review. By actively participating in these exercises, readers can gauge their mastery of the material and identify areas where additional study may be beneficial.

Practical Exercises for Comprehension Testing
Exercises are structured to bridge theory and application, guiding readers through practical scenarios where they can apply the knowledge they've gained. These exercises include hands-on tasks, reflective questions, and problem-solving activities that simulate real-world AI applications. Each exercise aims to deepen understanding and encourage readers to think critically about AI's principles and applications.

Example Exercise 1: Creating a Simple Decision Tree
- **Objective**: Guide readers through creating a basic decision tree model using a dataset.
- **Instructions**: Provide step-by-step instructions for choosing a dataset, defining decision criteria, and implementing the model using Python's Scikit-Learn library.
- **Reflection**: Encourage readers to assess the performance of their decision tree and think about real-life applications where such a model could be useful.

Example Exercise 2: Identifying Bias in Data Sets
- **Objective**: Help readers understand the impact of biased data on AI models.
- **Instructions**: Provide a sample dataset, and ask readers to analyze it for potential bias in terms of gender, age, or other categories.
- **Reflection**: Include questions to prompt readers to reflect on how this bias might affect model accuracy and fairness in real-world scenarios, highlighting ethical implications.

Each exercise is designed to challenge readers, encouraging a hands-on approach that reinforces theoretical concepts and fosters practical skills.

Summary Quizzes for Each Section

Quizzes provide a way to reinforce learning in a dynamic, engaging manner, allowing readers to assess their understanding immediately after completing a section. These quizzes include multiple-choice questions, true/false statements, and open-ended questions. The questions are structured to progressively cover key topics, beginning with foundational principles and advancing to more complex applications and ethical considerations.

Sample Quiz Questions

1. **Multiple Choice**: Which of the following best describes supervised learning?
    - A) Algorithms that learn from labeled data
    - B) Algorithms that learn from unlabeled data
    - C) Algorithms used solely for image recognition
    - D) Algorithms that require no human interaction
2. **True or False**: Deep learning is a subset of machine learning that involves the use of neural networks with multiple layers. (Answer: True)
3. **Open-Ended Question**: Describe one example of how AI can influence decision-making in healthcare. Discuss any ethical considerations that may arise from its use.

The quizzes are carefully crafted to balance technical knowledge with broader understanding, helping readers reflect on how AI concepts apply in various real-life contexts.

By completing these exercises and quizzes, readers can solidify their understanding, apply theoretical concepts, and gain practical experience in thinking critically about AI. This approach ensures a well-rounded learning experience, equipping readers with both the knowledge and skills to advance in their AI journey.